Managing
Student
Library
Employees

A Workshop for Supervisors

Michael D. Kathman
and Jane M. Kathman

Library Skills Series Number 1

Library Solutions Press · Berkeley, California

First Printing: January 1995

Graphics Editors: Catherine Dinnean and Stephanie Lipow

LIBRARY SOLUTIONS PRESS

Sales Office:	1100 Industrial Road, Suite 9 San Carlos, CA 94070
Fax orders:	415-594-0411
Telephone orders and inquiries:	510-841-2636
Web URL	http://www.internet-is.com/library/
Email	info@library-solutions.com
Editorial Office:	2137 Oregon Street, Berkeley, CA 94705
ISBN	1-882208-16-1

TABLE OF CONTENTS

LIST OF FIGURES

FOREWORD

By Anne Grodzins Lipow
Director, Library Solutions Institute and Press

About this book

In the early 1980s, I took the Kathmans' workshop on which this book is based. It would be an exaggeration to say that it changed my life, but it did make an enormous difference—at least at work. For years before that workshop, I was regarded as a good supervisor, managing a department of 12 full-time staff and about 10-15 student employees. I had learned a lot from Sheila Creth about supervising—especially about training and the value of written training plans.* Applying her principles to "regular" (or "career" or "permanent") staff of librarians and library technicians, I had a department that hummed. However, when it came to the student employees, it took a lot more of me (and a lot out of me) to ensure a smooth-running operation. But since my fellow supervisors experienced the same difficulties, it never occurred to me that things could go differently. Basically, I had the attitude that the Kathmans describe as common but bad: that essentially the students were doing me a favor by working for me. After all, they had more important things to do, like study hard, get good grades, and get on with their education. So when they overslept and came to work late, or needed extra time off to study for their final exams, or forgot to get a replacement who would take their shift (which may have included opening up the department first thing in the morning), or missed work–with apologies–because their job at the pizza parlor needed them that day, I would say "No problem." or "You're forgiven." Translation: "Students will be students; what else would you expect?!" As a result, I was forever training, filling in, training, juggling workloads and schedules, training, unraveling errors and correcting them, and, of course, training.

What I learned from the Kathmans is that there are several givens about student employees, such as their high turnover rate and their unsteady work schedules, that do not apply to permanent staff, and as a supervisor, I needed to take those differences into account when designing student employee jobs and managing their work. But in every respect, I should regard student employees as I did any other employee; I should expect of them the same quality and reliability in their work as I expect from other staff; and I should feel confident that their jobs are as essential as any other job in the library.

I came home from the workshop with a 180-degree turnabout in attitude and immediately began applying the Kathmans' ideas and methods. What a change! Turnover dropped dramatically as did "personnel problems"; productivity increased; training wasn't haphazard (i.e., at their convenience) so it took far less time to complete, and indeed training periods came to an end. And best of all, students behaved responsibly. They even seemed happy to be given the chance to work at a real job, just like regular adults do! And I moved up several notches in my effectiveness as a manager.

Now that I'm in a position to publish books that are the actual scripts of the workshops of expert trainers, you can understand why high on my list of candidates for this new series was the Kathmans'. Now, you, too, can "attend" their workshop and learn to be a very good student supervisor. Also, using this or the PLUS edition of this book (which includes diskettes containing files of the overheads), you can meet with other student supervisors and facilitate their training by leading them through the exercises and discussion.

Happy supervising!

A.G.L
January 1995

---

* If you don't know Sheila Creth's book *Effective On-the-Job Training,* (American Library Association, 1986), try to find a copy; it is currently out of print.

ABOUT THE AUTHORS

Michael D. Kathman is Director of Libraries and Media for the College of Saint Benedict and Saint John's University, two independent colleges. He is active at both the state and national level in library activities, having served as president of The Minnesota Library Association, the chair of the College Library Section of the Association of College and Research Libraries, and as the chair of the ACRL Planning Committee. Michael continues to serve on numerous state and national library committees and task forces. Also, Michael is mayor of Cold Spring, Minnesota and has served on the city council for the past 16 years.

Jane M. Kathman is professor of management at the College of Saint Benedict. She has received the Advisor of the Year Award from both the College of Saint Benedict and Saint John's University. Jane has received several grants for research and continued studies from the Bremer Foundation, the Northwest Area Foundation and the General Electric Corporation. With Michael, she has written articles and given workshops on conflict management. She is active on university and college committees and currently serves on the executive committee of the Saint John's Preparatory School Board of Regents.

Together Jane and Michael have been writing and giving workshops on Managing Student Employees for over 17 years. They have published articles in *College and Research Libraries*, *Journal of Academic Librarianship* and *Catholic Library World*. In 1994, they published CLIP NOTE #20: *Managing Student Employees*. They have given this workshop throughout the country for ACRL chapters, individual libraries and networks. They have also made presentations on this subject to bookstore and food service conferences, as well as to campus wide non library departments.

ABOUT THE SERIES

Paralleling our Internet Workshop Series, Library Skills Series will consist of workshops, in book form, of expert instructors who are teaching library staff what they need to know to stay competent in today's libraries. Generally, they cover practical how-to skills that are not easy to acquire elsewhere, including in library schools.

Other "workshops" planned in this series are:

Providing Excellent Service: Neutral Questioning and Customer Service Skills

How to Make Effective Presentations

Interviewing Techniques for Hiring the Right Person

How to Write Clear Instructions (for point-of-use directions, instructional brochures and training manuals)

How to Make Your Library Signs Work

A.G.L.

PREFACE

By the authors

A BIT OF BACKGROUND

We developed the earliest version of this workshop in 1980 as a continuing education course for the College and Research Libraries division of the American Library Association. Over the years we have given variations of the workshop to hundreds and hundreds of library staff—librarians and paraprofessionals—from public and academic libraries. We have also given the workshop for staff in non-library departments within academic institutions, as well as for food services and book store associations. The version presented here is designed primarily as a self-paced learning resource for the individual who directly supervises student library employees. This book can also serve as a model for the trainer responsible for training student supervisors. Throughout, the term "student supervisor" refers to the supervisor of student employees and not to student employees who have supervisory responsibility.

HOW TO GET THE MOST OUT OF THIS BOOK

1. Notice the Icons

a. Whenever you see this icon of an overhead projector, turn to Appendix 1: Presentation Slides, and look at the slide with the corresponding number (almost as if you were in our live workshop). Each slide is meant to highlight major points to be remembered.

Right now, for example, you might look at slide 1, the title slide, to be sure you are at the right workshop!

b. This icon indicates that you are at a point where YOUR ideas are wanted. Be sure to take the time to participate.

2. Tailor this workshop to YOUR situation

Keep in mind that nearly everything we say applies to many if not most library situations, but one size never fits all. If something we say doesn't "feel right" applied to your environment, ignore it. As in any workshop you take, what we cover must be adjusted to fit your own situation. Only you, the reader, can do that.

To help you customize the workshop to meet your needs, complete the Pre-workshop Exercise on page xi.

ACKNOWLEDGEMENTS

Considerable credit for this book goes to the staffs of Alcuin Library, St. John's University, and Clemens Library, The College of Saint Benedict, our testing grounds for many years, as well as to the hundreds of other participants in past workshops. All of them are day-to-day practitioners who generously shared with us the issues they grapple with, their expertise in how they have handled tough situations, and their ideas for making this workshop as useful as possible. Any omissions or errors, however, are fully our responsibility. As you make your way through this workshop, please note any passage that you feel needs to be clarified or changed and let us hear from you.

Michael Kathman   mkathman@csbsju.edu
Jane Kathman   jkathman@csbsju.edu

PRE-WORKSHOP EXERCISE

APPLYING WHAT YOU LEARN TO WHAT YOU DO.

A worthwhile technique for any workshop goer is to prepare for the workshop by having in mind situations in your own environment that you hope to improve because of what you learn in the workshop. Then, during the workshop, as you hear ideas and methods that are relevant to those situations, or to any others that are pertinent, jot them down so that you can be reminded of them when you are back on the job and ready to apply those methods to the situations you had hoped to improve. Finally, make a commitment before the workshop to find time shortly after the workshop to practice what you learned. Learning theorists say that unless you are primed for the workshop in this way, it is likely you will forget most of what you learned. The following exercise will enhance your chances of meeting your commitment.

Exercise 1: What's relevant to me

Keep this page handy to annotate throughout the workshop.
Use other side of this page as needed.

Describe one or two problems you have experienced, or are concerned you might experience, in relation to student employees that you would like to reduce, handle better next time, eliminate, avoid, or resolve. You will have the opportunity later in the workshop to deal specifically with the situations you note here.

Consider, for example, any of the following:
- an employee's behavior that irritates you
- a situation that caught you by surprise
- a type of problem that if reduced would make your job a lot easier
- a chronic supervisory problem that makes your life miserable
- another supervisor's predicament you've observed and want to avoid
- a dilemma you've encountered and cannot resolve
- or any other!

Problem 1	Good ideas
Problem 2	Good ideas

What's relevant to me (continued notes)

Other good ideas from the workshop:

THE WORKSHOP

Why this workshop?

As a supervisor of student employees, your goal is to achieve consistency in hiring student employees who are easy to train, easy to work with, reliable, competent, and long-term enough to have made your investment in their development worthwhile. Without careful planning and a fair amount of knowledge about hiring, training, and supervising, the odds that you will realize your goal are slim. That's because of the high turnover among student employees; their inexperience in working at a real job (for many, yours is their first job); their minimal knowledge about the library; and in many cases YOUR lack of formal training as a supervisor. Often, too, student employees seem to lack a real interest in the work because they know the job is a temporary expedient enabling them to finance their education.

These barriers to your success as a supervisor may appear insurmountable and cause you frustrations, even demoralization. This workshop is intended to assist you in overcoming those barriers and in reaching your goal. It will help you understand the special nature of student employment and provide you with practical ideas and techniques for successfully hiring, training, supervising, and evaluating student employees.

MODULE  1

THE NATURE OF STUDENT EMPLOYMENT

A. PERSPECTIVES ON STUDENT EMPLOYEES

1. *Some facts about student employees*

   - Student employees account for about 9% of a library's personnel budget in large academic and research libraries, and about 13% in college libraries *(see refs. 1 & 33 in Appendix 2)*. If they were to be replaced with full-time employees, the cost would be two to three times as much, depending on the wage rates. Wage rates vary greatly among institutions. In general, student employees are paid lower wages than full-time library employees, and most student employees do not receive fringe benefits.

   - Because students are at the bottom of the organization's hierarchy, they are often not viewed as a valuable resource. This also means that student supervision is often not valued. Too often the responsibilities of student supervision are not recorded or sufficiently acknowledged in paraprofessional or professional job descriptions and are not commented on during the supervisor's evaluation.

   - If the library does not have a clear, well-worked-out plan for managing student employees, it can take much longer to select, train, and evaluate four 10-hour-per-week student employees than it does one full-time employee!

2. *What's special about student employees?*

   Student employees are not replacements for full-time people. If the category did not exist, we would probably invent it because:

   - Much of the work that libraries require is best done by part-time workers, and students constitute an outstanding pool of potential part-time workers to fill those needs. For example,
     a. they are available to work at odd hours, thus enabling the library to be open for extended hours
     b. they are available to work for brief stints

c. they have special language or technical skills needed in libraries, though not at full time.

- By performing the more routine work in the library, student employees enable librarians and support staff to concentrate on more complex tasks.

Since they are both library users and library service providers, student employees, on the one hand, can be an excellent source of advice about how to improve services, and on the other hand, can help spread a good word and accurate information about the library among their peers, parents, and other patrons.

3. *Your attitude about "problem employees"*

When looking to change a "problem employee," organizations would do well to look first to their management practices rather than to their employee. Most problem employees will respond to improved management. Or, to put it another way, you'll get further getting an employee to change behavior by focusing on management rather than on the employee. The following exercises will help you reflect on your opinions about student employees, and, depending on your answers, may suggest areas you'll want to discuss further with colleagues.

Exercise 2: Examining your attitudes about student employees

Which of the following statements do you agree with more?

a. The student employee is doing me a favor working for me, since a student has more important or pressing things to do, like taking classes and exams, and studying. So I must make allowances and relax normal work standards.

b. The jobs reserved for students in my department are part-time positions consisting of important library work. The student worker must adhere to many of the same standards of quality work as other library employees, such as meeting work schedules or completing work within expected time frames.

I agree more with   a. _____   b. _____

If your answer tends toward "a," then your attitude may be an underlying reason for some of the problems you are experiencing as a supervisor and coordinator of workflow. By the end of this workshop, we hope you will agree with "b."

Exercise 3: The importance of YOU, the supervisor

a. Question:
The same student can be an asset under one supervisor and a liability under another. How can this be explained?

Your ideas:

Answer: If you answered "It's the supervisor who makes the difference," you are right! It is important that you appreciate how critical you are to the success of the student employee's performance.

b. Proposition:
Student employees, as all other employees, demonstrate the Pygmalion effect: they perform to the level of their supervisor's expectations.

Your observations:

B. STUDENT EMPLOYEES AS PERIPHERAL WORKERS

1. The literature

What motivates most employees to do a good job, the management literature says, is directly related to their commitment to long-term careers in an organization or profession *(refs. 38 & 54)*. The literature also reports that their behavior as employees is influenced by their perception of how their personal goals can be achieved through their workplace or occupation *(ref. 24)*. These conclusions are drawn from studies done primarily on full-time workers. On both counts—commitment to the organization and the belief they can achieve their personal goals through the organization—student employees would score very low. So we can learn very little about managing student employees from most of the management literature.

However, Gannon and Morse *(refs. 18 & 42)* explain what they term "peripheral workers," a category which most closely fits the student employee. Their findings help us understand the student's perspective. They offer useful concepts to assist us in our performance as supervisors, which in turn result in the student employee's improved performance.

2. Characteristics of peripheral workers

Gannon and Morse researched both full- and part-time employees in several service industries, including grocery store workers, retail clerks, and bank tellers. They found the following characteristics:

a. They have a partial commitment to the organization.

b. They view work not as a career, but as a job.

c. They regard their job as secondary to other, more important activities.

This description closely parallels characteristics of student employees, who typically view their work in libraries as a job secondary to more important activities. Their primary goal is to finance their education, which in turn will lead to a career elsewhere. Many student employees perceive that their educational and career goals are not related to on-campus employment and have at best a partial commitment to such work.

Viewing student employees in this context of peripheral workers can help explain the negative job attitudes such as those exhibited by poor performance and productivity, absenteeism, and tardiness.

3. Motivating peripheral workers

Full-time employees are generally motivated to do good work because they foresee that such an investment will be rewarded over time. That motivator-from-within is a help to their supervisors. By contrast, as a supervisor of student employees, you cannot expect those you supervise to have this internal motivator. According to Gannon and Morse, that is because their jobs in the library seem irrelevant (peripheral) to their main educational and career goals.

Fortunately, all employees—whether full-time and long-term or temporary and peripheral—respond to external motivators provided by their workplace. For full-time career employees, these motivators reinforce and complement their internal motivators. However, for peripheral employees, their desire to do well may hinge entirely on these *external* motivators.

The literature describes many techniques that supervisors can use to create a climate that fosters positive job attitudes and the desire to do well. The challenge for supervisors of peripheral workers, including student employees, is to create such a climate despite the conditions mentioned earlier that can contribute to negative job attitudes.

In particular, it is our premise that student employees will overcome those inhibitors and will want to perform well in a climate in which the following motivators are an integral part of their work environment and experience:

- supervisor makes clear what is expected on the job
- supervisor demonstrates the conviction that the student employee's job is important
- supervisor applies rules consistently and fairly
- supervisor expects student employee to accept responsibility for an assigned area of work and to be accountable for the quality, quantity, and completion of that work
- supervisor designs tasks that ensure continued acquisition of new knowledge and skills
- supervisor acknowledges high-quality performance through rewards

In the following modules, you will learn how to create this climate for your student employees by incorporating these motivators into the major activities of managing student employees:

- Hiring
- Training
- Supervising and Evaluating

Accordingly, you will learn techniques to apply during these processes, which accomplish the following:

- clarify expectations
- demonstrate the importance of the student employee's work
- ensure unbiased treatment of staff
- inculcate a sense of responsibility, accountability, and accomplishment

- support learning more about the job, the department, and the library
- recognize, acknowledge, and reward quality work

C. SUMMARY OF MODULE 1

Key ideas I want to remember about student employment:

MODULE 2 HIRING THE RIGHT PERSON

A. LAYING THE FOUNDATION: THE JOB DESCRIPTION

If you have a written job description for your student employee, have it handy for this module.

At the heart of a good workplace are good job descriptions. A well-written job description of each student employee's job is a must. For you, it provides the context for the training, supervision, and evaluation of your employee. For the student employee, it communicates clearly the basic duties and expectations of the job.

1. *Job description vs. job announcement*

   The job description is not to be confused with the job announcement. The latter is usually brief—a short statement listing two or three major components of the job and the required skills, as well as information that would attract desirable candidates. The job description is an outline of the duties the job entails, including any other information that applicants need to know to decide whether the job is suitable for them. See *Figure 1* and *Figure 2* for a sample of each.

   A job description should include the following:
   - The components of the job
   - Skills and knowledge required
   - Skills and knowledge desirable
   - Work schedule requirements (if any)
   - An idea of workloads to be accomplished within specific time frames (if any)

2. *The contents of a job description*

   The job description should reflect not only the skills that are needed but also the time required to do the job. For example, in *Figure 2*, which describes a serials assistant job in a small college library, notice the work schedule requirement of three to four hours a day between 10:00am and 2:00pm. The reason for this time frame is that the mail does not come in until about 9:30am; and in order that the journals be shelved within two hours of receipt, the work must be completed before 2:00pm. So it makes no sense to have the student there before the mail arrives, or after 2:00pm.

Figure 1

SAMPLE JOB ANNOUNCEMENT FOR A STUDENT EMPLOYEE

Wanted: Reliable and diligent student to work in the Library Serials Department

Position: Serials Assistant

Basic duties: Process newly received journal and newspaper issues using automated system; shelve and display new issues; refer problem receipts

Skills required: Ability to sustain accurate keying and attention to detail in performance of repetitive tasks over 3–4 hour period

Skills desired: Knowledge of a foreign language, knowledge of Library of Congress classification system

Work schedule: 12–15 hours/week; 3–4 hours in a day; between 10am – 2pm

Pay: $x.xx/hour

Benefits: Enjoyable workplace; learn new skills; advancement opportunities; excellent basis for future job references

Figure 2

SAMPLE JOB DESCRIPTION FOR A STUDENT EMPLOYEE

JOB TITLE: Serials Assistant; 12–15 hours/week

- Process newly received periodicals and newspapers: record receipt in automated Serials Control System (match title and issue to correct record, enter coded and textual information); mark physical issue appropriately
    Skills required: accurate keying, 50 words/minute
    Skills desired: knowledge of a foreign language
    Workload (after training): 20–30 records per hour

- Shelve certain materials in call number range G through N; shelve certain materials alphabetically by title
    Skills required: discerning and sustained attention to detail
    Skills desired: knowledge of how to shelve in Library of Congress call number order
    Workload (after training): shelve 100 incoming issues per 4-hour work shift

- Display new issues of selected popular journals in browsing area between 10am and 2pm daily, 1–2 hours per day
    Work schedule required: 3–4 hours in a day, between 10am and 2pm

- Forward problem receipts to Serials Troubleshooter
    Skills required:
        ability to recognize incoming issues that do not match with records
        ability to communicate clearly

It is important that the student be able to complete the job during the work shift or during a work week. Describing a realistic workload in the job description pays off later: for you, the supervisor, it helps focus your training; for student employees, it results in their being able to see measurable accomplishments that in turn will increase motivation to accomplish more. The supervisor should be able to do all of the responsibilities required in the job before asking a student to do them. You would be surprised how many student jobs cannot be done in the time allotted as listed in the job description.

Avoid the temptation to put everything required in the whole area into the job description.

It is important that as supervisor you be clear about your expectations for the position. Do not expect a student to know every library policy and to be able to perform every duty in an area. List only the three or four most important and realistic expectations you have for a position. If you can clearly identify them, selecting, training, and evaluating student employees will be made much easier.

3. *Your student employee's job description*

Exercise 4: Sketch out your student employee's job description

Student employee's job title: _____

Major job tasks	Skills required/desired	Work load	Schedule requirements

B. INTERVIEWING AND SELECTING

With a clear understanding of the job for which you are hiring, you have an objective basis for weeding, interviewing, and selecting applicants.

1. *The application*

   Application forms can be very helpful in identifying the right student for the job. Although many institutions have institution-wide student application forms, you may find that forms designed by the library that specifically address library-related issues may be best for you. For example, given both the long hours of service and the need to be open during holidays, it is helpful to know whether students will be around during academic vacations. Extracurricular interests should be noted during an interview and when scheduling hours. During the interview, asking about extracurricular interests may give applicants the opportunity to talk about their ability to work as a member of a team. Some supervisors have found that particular extra-curricular activities or major areas of study call for skills that are highly compatible with those needed on the job. Once the decision has been made to hire the student, that person's extracurricular activities might form the basis of a discussion when scheduling a student. For student athletes, practice and game times are known well in advance and should be considered when working with a student to draw up a schedule. The same is true for students involved in drama, debate, the newspaper, or other similar activities.

   An uncomplicated application form that elicits some of the information you are looking for will help you choose the applicants you wish to interview from among the total pool.

   See *Figure 3* for a sample application.

Figure 3

SAMPLE APPLICATION FOR LIBRARY STUDENT EMPLOYMENT

Name_____

Campus Phone # _____

Campus Address _____

Home Address _____

Year in College (circle one): Fr So Jr Sr   GPA_____

Major/Minor _____

Extracurricular Interests (please check):

___ Clubs, Name_____

___ Sports, Name_____

___ Volunteer Work, Name_____

___ Other, Name_____

Previous job experience:

Skills (Please check appropriate items):

___Art work   ___Media equipment   ___Computer skills   ___Book mending

___Filing   ___Word processing   ___Languages (Specify) _____

___Spread sheet   ___Data base   ___Other:_____

Do you prefer to work:

____ With clients at a public service desk   ____ In a technical area   ____No preference

____ As part of a team   ____ Alone   ____ No preference

Are you able to work during: ____ Evenings   ____ Weekends

____ Winter vacation   ____ Spring vacation   ____ Long weekends

Check semester(s) able to work: ____ Fall   ____ Spring   ____ Summer

_____   _____

    Signature   Date

FOR LIBRARY USE ONLY

Interviewer's Comments: _____

This student has been hired in _____ Department

by _____   Date _____

9

2. *Preparing for the interview*

Interviews, preferably conducted by the immediate supervisor, are of great assistance in selecting student employees. Supervisors can gain valuable information that supplements a paper application. The goal is to find the best fit between supervisor, employee, and job.

Interviews also provide the supervisor with the opportunity to communicate the importance of the job and the person in the job and their expectations to the prospective employee. Thus, interviews are an important first step in motivating an employee.

a. Forms for interviewing

To ensure that you cover the issues you want to cover, have a written plan. You might want to start with a checklist, such as the one in *Figure 4*.

Better than a checklist is a plan that relates the job to skills you are looking for and performance standards you require. This can be done by using parts of the job description and building upon them. A form that represents the categories you would want to consider might look like this:

Duties / Tasks / Standards	Related skills / Knowledge / Abilities

To do this properly, you need to be aware of the sort of skills, knowledge, and abilities you'll be looking for. Take a moment to think about this in Exercise 5.

Exercise 5:
What makes a successful employee in YOUR department?

List three main characteristics that a student employee would need to possess to be successful in your unit:

1.

2.

3.

Figure 4

SAMPLE CHECKLIST OF INFORMATION TO ELICIT FROM CANDIDATE

Critical Information

___ Hours available to work (meets department's needs)

___ Outside obligations that could affect schedule

___ Health (including ADA) issues that may affect scheduling, assignment of duties

Technical Skills

___ Handwriting on application

___ Use of, and familiarity with, library

People-to-People Skills

___ Congenial and pleasing manner

___ Appearance and voice

Work Attitudes

___ Abilities and willingness to work

___ Cooperative attitude

___ Interest in people and books

___ Dependable

Pertinent Facts

___ Academic standing

___ Year in school

___ Special interests

___ Previous work experience

___ Possesses skills which are helpful for position

___ Holds another job

___ Outside interests and activities

___ Financial aid received

___ Reasons for application

Information to give to candidate

___ Your expectations (two-way street)

___ The importance of job

b. Questions to ask the candidates

You are now ready to prepare questions that will elicit useful responses from the candidates. The best questions are those that ask the candidates to talk about their experience in situations comparable to yours, rather than what they might do in those situations.

For example, if your job calls for routine, accurate work, do not ask "How do you like routine work? Are you able to maintain accuracy throughout a four-hour period?" Instead ask questions such as "Tell me about a time when you did repetitive work that required a high degree of accuracy." "Think about a time when you made more errors doing a job than was acceptable. What happened?" "Can you recall a time when after a long day of work your energy flagged and you began to make errors you normally wouldn't make?"

Exercise 6: Choosing the right words

In preparing questions for interview, do not use loaded, negative words such as "dull," or "boring," as in "Are you able to maintain accuracy throughout a four-hour period of boring work?"

What's wrong with using such words?

What words would work better?

Repetitive, routine, detailed
Some possibilities:

If your job calls for working with the public, don't ask "How do you handle an angry person?" Rather, "Tell me about a time when [a customer in your past job; a teammate] got overly angry with you. How did you handle it?"

Be prepared to ask the interviewee for a more positive experience if they report a negative one, and vice versa. You are looking for what they learned from their negative experiences and the attitudes they convey about their positive experiences.

Also, for the candidate you eventually hire, you are laying the foundation for and conveying information about what will be expected of that person on the job.

Exercise 7: Practice devising interview questions

Following are some common performance standards expected of student employees and the abilities required to do the tasks. For each one, draft one interview question.

Reliable

Prompt

Cooperative/Team player

Courteous and respectful toward clients

Problem-solving

Accurate filing/keying/shelving

Exercise 8: Prepare the interview for your next student employee

Referring to your student employee's job description as well as the checklist in *Figure 4*, use the form below to assign skills and abilities to some of the required job duties. Include relevant characteristics and skills you are looking for (Exercise 5) as well as standards you want met (Exercise 7). Then draft one question that corresponds to each of the skills you've listed. (The same skills may be needed for more than one duty.)

Job duties	Related skills/knowledge/abilities	Interview questions
1.		
2.		
3.		
4.		
5.		

3. *Conducting the interview*

The interview should be held in an area that is private and free from distractions. Hold phone calls and other interruptions.

The interview should be relatively brief, 20–30 minutes.

Establish rapport. Offer a brief welcome.

Say a few words—no more than a minute or two—about the department and the job. Now is not the time to go into detail about either one. If you do, you will likely be coaching the applicant about the kind of answers you want to hear. Instead of "This is a very busy place with lots of deadline work to be done, such as...", simply state the major functions of your unit, and then begin asking the applicant the questions you've planned, including getting to how the applicant performs in a busy environment. For example, "Tell me about a time when you had more work to do than you could finish by the deadline." Or, "Describe a job or activity you were responsible for when there were competing demands." Let the applicant do most of the talking. Keep your participation to questions. (If you do most of the talking, you're not listening and you're not getting information from the applicant.)

During the interview, jot down notes that will help you remember the candidate or remind you later of why you did or did not choose the candidate.

When you are done with your questions, ask whether the applicant has any questions. If you have stuck to our guideline and said little about the job, what would you think of an applicant who had no questions about job specifics? You would be right to be concerned that if hired, this person might not ask questions about things that were not clear.

At the close of the interview, inform the applicant when to expect a decision.

4. *Selecting the right applicant*

Decide on a scoring system (for example, a five-point scale) that signifies how well the candidate did on each question. This will enable you to compare applicants more easily and objectively; or, if you are hiring on the spot, it will enable you to decide based on a minimal score.

5. *The employment agreement*

An employment agreement, which the chosen candidates read and sign, can be an important means of underscoring the expectations that were raised in the interview and informing them of other important matters that were not previously covered. See *Figure 5* for a sample employment agreement.

C. SUMMARY OF MODULE 2

Key ideas I learned about the hiring process:

Figure 5

SAMPLE EMPLOYMENT AGREEMENT

Employee's name_____ Date _____

Schedule for _____ (term)   _____ (year)

The library agrees to employ you through the coming term, provided the requirements set here are met.

This schedule is for the entire term. If you need to make changes see your immediate supervisor.

Monday: _____

Tuesday: _____

Wednesday: _____

Thursday: _____

Friday: _____

Saturday: _____

Sunday: _____

Substitutes for planned absences: You may have another library student employee substitute for you if you have filled out a Student Substitute Form. We expect you to locate a substitute using the Student Staff Directory as distributed. If you are not able to locate a substitute after making a serious effort or in case of a grave emergency, notify your immediate supervisor or the librarian on duty and inform them of your difficulty.

I understand and accept the following responsibilities:

• To work the above-scheduled hours for the entire term
• To work equivalent hours (to be arranged) for exam periods
• To arrange for a substitute (according to stated procedures) or to notify a librarian in case of an emergency
• To become familiar with the Student Personnel Manual
• To master in a reasonable time period the requirements of my assignment

Signed:_____   Date:_____

MODULE 3 TRAINING

A. ORIENTATION

1. *The big picture*

Providing general information—"the big picture"—about the library sets the tone for the employment experience. A positive beginning starts the student employee off with a positive job attitude toward employment, coworkers, supervisors, and the institution. How this orientation is done depends on the size of the institution. In small institutions all student employees could be included. In large institutions you might want to include only new students, and in very large institutions, orientation may have to be done at the departmental level only.

Some institutions have a continuous hiring process, while others tend to hire most of their student employees in the fall. If there are large numbers of student employees added during the year, general orientations may need to be conducted throughout the year. This depends on the local circumstances in each library.

The general orientation should convey the importance of the library within the larger community and describe its major accomplishments. It also should include a statement of why student employees are important to the institution. The mission of the library and how student employees assist in meeting the mission should be clearly stated. In smaller institutions this orientation could be given by the director of libraries. In larger institutions if the director is not available, it should be given by someone the student employees recognize as a person with authority in the library. A technique used in larger libraries is to gather new employees in large groups to receive information that applies to all areas of the library, and then break into smaller groups for information about specific departments.

Another part of the general orientation should be an introduction to the general policies and procedures affecting all student employees: how to get paid, contractual obligations, what to do in emergencies, and so forth.

Finally, an introduction to key staff and how they can assist student employees (what they do) should be included.

It is worthwhile to brainstorm with your fellow supervisors about what to include in your general orientation. Your goal should be to devise a program that is both upbeat and professional. Perceptions and impressions about your department's work environment may very likely be formed during this initial orientation.

Figure 6 is an example of a general orientation agenda:

Figure 6

SAMPLE STUDENT EMPLOYEE GENERAL ORIENTATION IN A SMALL COLLEGE LIBRARY

12:30 – 1:00   Registration and Welcome
            Director welcomes new employees and talks about the mission and goals of the library

1:00 – 1:30   Everything you always wanted to know about what the staff does but were afraid to ask

1:30 – 2:00   Specific topic based on issues that came up in the past year
            • Teamwork
            • Overview of the library as a service organization
            • Job expectations

2:00 – 2:30   General policies and procedures for student employees

2:30 – 4:00   Department training sessions

4:00 – 4:30   Mingle with the old and meet the new

Pop and Cookies

2. *Departmental orientation*

The departmental orientation parallels what happens at the library-wide level, except that it deals with *departmental* goals, staff, and issues.

Policies and procedures specific to the department and not covered in the general orientation should be presented.

Exercise 9: Planning the Orientation

What key concepts would you convey in an introductory orientation to the library?

What would you say about why the work is important?

How would you describe the library's mission?

Whom does the work serve?

What topics would you cover in an introduction to YOUR unit?

B. JOB TRAINING

Training can be accomplished by the use of handbooks, computer-assisted instruction (CAI), videos, experienced student employees, hands-on practice, and so forth. However, the immediate supervisor should be a key player in the training process.

There are four main reasons for this:

- the supervisor begins to establish a good working relationship with the student employee.
- the supervisor should know the job better than anyone else.
- the supervisor knows what has worked well with students in past training experiences.
- the supervisor can set the tone for the quality and quantity of work expected and develop a communication pattern with student employees.

1. *Start with a written training plan*

   A written training plan will serve as a guide for both you and your trainee. There is no one right format for a written training plan. It can be a checklist, prose, flowchart, time line, or a combination of these. For the purposes of this workshop, let's work with the checklist format.

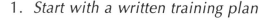

For each task, you will make a checklist of what training is needed, who should do the training (in some cases, you may not be the best person), what written materials support the training, estimated length of training, and how you will know when training is complete. If you have designed your student job well, training will be completed within a relatively short period of time after hiring.

Figure 7 is an example of such a checklist:

Figure 7

SAMPLE WRITTEN TRAINING PLAN (CHECKLIST FORMAT)

Key responsibility(ies): Maintain pamphlet file; order supplies

Training checklist:	trainer	supporting materials	length of training	training completed
Job Task 1: <u>File pamphlets</u> *purpose of file* *speed to aim for* *degree of accuracy to aim for* *filing rules* *define terms* *show examples* *give practice exercise*	me	pamphlets Manual of Procedures	6-8 hours	accurate filing for 2 consecutive weeks
Job Task 2: <u>Order supplies</u> *importance of keeping* *supplies stocked* *where kept* *forms needed* *"low stock" alert*	me Sally (Purchasing)	Supplies Catalog sample forms	2-3 hours	accurately initiate and process 5 supply orders

Exercise 10: Your training checklist

Using the form below, fill in the columns for two tasks you will be training your student employee to perform.

Key responsibility(ies): _____

Training checklist:	trainer	supporting materials	length of training	training completed
Job Task 1: _____				
Job Task 2: _____				

a. Order of training

What to train for first? That's up to you to decide. If you have a lot of time before the student needs to be up to speed on the job, perhaps start with emergency procedures, or start with the easiest thing to do and build on that. If the student must be productive on day one, start with the most frequently experienced situation, or begin with the task that must be done right away, even though it won't arise often. You can give a copy of a written training plan, such as the one you started in Exercise 10, to your student employee and use it to check off each item in the checklist as the training is completed. That way, no matter where you start the training, or despite inevitable interruptions, rearrangements, or amendments, both you and the student employee will know what training remains.

b. Creating external motivators

The very existence of a written training plan constitutes an external motivator. It carries an important message to the new employee: the fact that you took the time to think about the job seriously enough to create that plan conveys how important the job must be. The new employee, in turn, begins to build a sense of pride in the job and a desire to do well.

Also, you should use each training session as an opportunity to communicate your expectations of how the job should be done. For example, if you are concerned with timeliness, dependability, what you want accomplished in a two-hour period, or that you want the clients to be treated with respect, say so.

2. *The training session*

a. A two-way process

The training session should be interactive, a two-way process, involving oral instruction and demonstrations that include both supervisor and employee doing the tasks. Supervisors should be mindful about encouraging student employees to ask questions.

b. Written instructions

Your oral training should be supported with written materials: descriptions of what the student employee needs to know to do a good job, as well as all applicable library policies. These should be in an easy-to-find format. Part of the training can be to show the employee how to use the appropriate written resource to look up what has just been taught and to find information not covered in detail because of infrequent need.

c. Testing your training

Some type of feedback mechanism should be included in your training program. Some supervisors "test" training about three weeks into the employee's term. This can be done through observation, paper and pencil tests, or checking the quality of work. Others use survey forms to determine where students feel they are well trained, where they are uncertain, and what they would like to learn. It is important to understand that what is being "tested" is the training process, how successful it has been thus far, and what more needs to be done. You are not expecting a perfect performance from the trainee during the training period!

In Figures 8, 9, 10, and 11 are examples of forms, adapted from Lake Forest College, used in training student employees in the circulation department.

3. *Giving criticism and praise*

During training it is important that mistakes made be regarded as good, not bad. You should think of them as opportunities to correct misimpressions, fill in omissions, or revisit a complex task. And it is important that you address those mistakes as close to the time they were made as possible.

It is equally important that you reinforce correct behavior during training with praise—again, as close to the time they were noticed as possible.

Whether you are giving criticism or praise, describe the action or behavior or aspect of their work that you saw; do not use loaded adjectives that ascribe an attitudes or motive to the student. You can see your employees' work; you cannot see their attitude. However, you may describe *your* feelings about their behavior or the impact their work had on you. Also, be specific in your descriptions, not general.

Wrong way	*Right way*
That was a great job you did!	I was extremely impressed that you keyed 50 records in only 20 minutes without making one error. That's been done only once before since I've been here!
You sure are sloppy.	The type-overs and erasures in this letter that you typed give it a messy look. Show me how you are making corrections; let's find a better way...

Figure 8

SAMPLE ORIENTATION RECORD

LIBRARY CIRCULATION DEPARTMENT

Employee's name:_____   Date:_____

Initial   Date

__   _____ Application completed

__   _____ Schedule sheets (2 copies) completed

__   _____ Picture taken

__   _____ Orientation packet

__   _____ Assigned to:_____
            (experienced student) with Training Progress Report form

__   _____ Final exam schedule (to be completed and returned)

__   _____ Shelf reading test (after 2 weeks)

__   _____ Library policies and procedures test (after 3 weeks)

_____

ITEMS RETURNED

__   _____ Circulation training checklist

__   _____ Training progress report form

__   _____ Final exam schedule

Adapted from Lake Forest College

Figure 9

SAMPLE CIRCULATION TRAINING CHECKLIST

Trainee's name: _____   Date:_____

Trainer's name:_____

Initial Date

___ ____   Charging/discharging books

___ ____   Light pen, use and labels

___ ____   Books returned without labels

___ ____   Overdues problem report forms and fines

___ ____   Missing books and search request forms

___ ____   Time cards

___ ____   Typing light pen labels

___ ____   Reserve check-out slips

___ ____   Reserve organization (open and closed)

___ ____   Sign-ins for off-campus users

___ ____   Security system

___ ____   Telephone procedures

___ ____   Assignment sheets

___ ____   Shelving and different types of preshelving areas

___ ____   Pickups and pickup areas

___ ____   Keeping statistics on pickups

___ ____   Periodical use sheets

___ ____   Referrals of reference, policy, and other questions

Adapted from Lake Forest College

Figure 10

SAMPLE TRAINING PROGRESS REPORT

Library Circulation Department

CIRCULATION ASSISTANT

Trainee's name:_____ Date:_____

Initial

__ I have read and understand the Student Personnel Manual.
(You will be held responsible for the contents; do not initial until you have read it.)

__ I know I should check IDs, and I am aware of which people are allowed to borrow books.

__ I know how to use the computer to charge and discharge books.

__ I know that I should check the date stamp with the due date on the computer before stamping a book.

__ I know that if I cannot find a book in the online catalog that has been returned, or it comes up "BOOK NOT CHARGED," I should ask for help or put the book on the "problem book" cart

__ I know where the Overdue Complaint Forms are and what their purpose is.

__ I know I cannot accept money for fines.

__ I know what a "prior save" is and what to do with one.

__ I know how to recall books.

__ I know how to transfer telephone calls.

__ I know when to refer people/questions to a librarian.

__ My shelf reading assignment is_____.

__ I know how to find and check out reserve materials.

__ I know the difference between open and closed reserve.

__ I know how to label books for the light pen.

__ I know where the daily assignment sheets are posted and how to initial the ones I have done.

__ I know how to work all three copy machines including how to clear a misfeed and how to replace the paper.

__ I know where all the keys are kept and the purpose of each.

__ I know how to punch in and out on my time card.

__ I know who handles interlibrary loans and how to refer someone to them.

Adapted from Lake Forest College

Figure 11

SAMPLE TEST OF TRAINING

Answer each question below as completely as possible.

1. What is the phone number for the Circulation Desk?
    What is the phone number for the Circulation Office?

2. Who is the Head Librarian?

3. What are the noncirculating collections in the library?

4. To deactivate the Tattle-Tape system, one must move
    the switch:
    (circle letter)   a. up   b. down

5. Lost and Found items are kept where?

6. Where are the pencil sharpeners located?

7. How are the group study rooms reserved?

8. What are the hours of the library?

9. Where is the music library?

10. Where is the recall/hold shelf?

11. Where is the library's collection of phone books?

12. Where is the microcomputer lab?

13. Where are the bathrooms?

14. How many times can a book be renewed?

15. What do you do with interlibrary loan requests?

16. What is the fine for an overdue reserve book?

Exercise 11: Practice giving specific criticism and praise

Wrong   *How would you make it right?*

You were extremely rude
to the client.

You always monopolize
our staff meetings.

You are SO creative!

C. SUMMARY OF MODULE 3

Key ideas I learned about the training process:

MODULE 4 SUPERVISING AND EVALUATING

Supervision is the responsibility to select, direct, coordinate, motivate, and evaluate the efforts of employees. Effective supervision of student employees includes understanding student employees' goals as students and relating those goals to their jobs in the library.

A. FUNCTIONS OF A STUDENT SUPERVISOR

1. *Clarify nature of tasks*

    a. Define and describe task; explain why it is done

    b. Provide good training

    c. Solicit student employee's ideas

2. *Reduce roadblocks for successful completion of task*

    a. Be sure student employee understands what is expected

    b. Introduce employee to the larger unit and its personnel

    c. Provide written materials: guidelines, lists, instructions

3. *Monitor continuing performance*

    a. Be a role model

    b. Stay in touch with employee

    c. Provide a work environment that fosters continued success

4. *Transmit information up and down the hierarchy*

    a. Represent the needs and accomplishments of your student employees to your supervisor

    b. Communicate to your student employees news, desires, policy changes, and trends emanating from library administration

18

B. SUPERVISORY STYLES

Research on leadership in management tells us that there is no one best way to supervise *(see ref. 9 in Appendix 2)*. Supervisors bring a wide range of supervisory styles to their jobs. These styles are influenced by the supervisor's personality, learning style, and previous work experience. Also, it is appropriate that an individual supervisor use different styles depending on the situation, the type of work to be done, and the people involved.

The four common supervisory styles that work best are
- directive
- participative
- achievement-oriented
- supportive

The *directive* supervisor emphasizes formal activities such as planning, organizing, and measuring work performance. For the student supervisor, this type of supervision includes giving student employees specific guidelines about how to do tasks, scheduling work, and clearly explaining to employees what is expected of them. The directive style is most needed during the orientation and training of student employees.

The *participative* supervisor consults with employees to gather their suggestions for use in making a decision. For example, a student supervisor might include the students when planning weekend work hours or changes in how on-the-job training might be improved. In some cases, after setting limits, the student supervisor may even leave the decision up to the student employees.

The *achievement-oriented* supervisor sets challenging goals and high expectations for employees. Student supervisors using this style might communicate how many books are expected to be shelved in two hours or how many books should be cataloged in a week.

The *supportive* supervisor expresses concern for the employees' well-being and creates an emotionally supportive climate. Management research indicates that employees whose jobs involve routine tasks perform better and are more satisfied under supportive supervisions *(ref. 25)*. Most student employees in libraries perform routine and repetitive tasks and need supportive supervision.

1. *What does it mean to be a supportive supervisor?*

   a. Clarify the nature of the work

      This is usually done through the orientation and training process. A supportive supervisor takes the time to explain:
      - why the work is important.
      - why things are done certain ways.
      - what happens if the work is done incorrectly.

   b. Give responsibility

      Supportive supervisors give employees the responsibility to complete work that meets clear expectations. This means employees are given the freedom to perform the work without excessive checking.

   c. Show concern for the employee

      This means the supervisor is willing to seek and listen to employees' suggestions. For student employees, it is important that the work performed be related to future career aspirations. Supportive supervisors can indicate how skills (computer, interpersonal, attentiveness to detail, etc.) practiced in library work are applicable in future careers.

2. *The relationship between job design and motivation*

   Management studies indicate that supervisors who design jobs around the core dimensions of a job can increase both the quality of the employee's work experience and their productivity. Also, designing jobs based on these core dimensions can increase the employee's motivation to do a good job. That is, by building into the student employee's job these core elements, you are also building external motivators. The following five dimensions determine a particular job's motivational potential: *(ref. 20)*

   a. Skill variety

      Try to plan for diverse activities and skills to be utilized. This helps decrease monotony and gives the student a sense of competence.

b. Task identity

Whenever possible, plan student work modules for a day or week when a whole piece of work can be completed, for example, shelving two carts of books in a two-hour period of time. This allows students to identify their own work effort and provides them a sense of accomplishment.

c. Task significance

Explain how the work students do affects other people who work in or use the library. This increases the importance of the job.

d. Autonomy

Allow students to exercise some discretion and control over the job. You may explain what needs to be accomplished in a particular day or week, but they can plan the order and be more responsible for the outcome of the work.

e. Feedback

Students are used to getting feedback regularly in classes. Conveying information frequently regarding their performance, both positive and negative, will reinforce your expectations.

Management research has proven that supervisors who utilize the five core job dimensions in planning work and designing jobs benefit from having employees who are highly motivated, perform well, and experience low absenteeism.

C. EVALUATION OF PERFORMANCE

Performance appraisal is not only an evaluative process but also a tool to stimulate communication between the student and the supervisor, a mechanism for reaffirming or setting new goals, and an opportunity to identify skills which can be improved.

Evaluation is a continuous process. Both the quality and quantity of a student's work should be evaluated at regular intervals, not just at the end of the term. Praise for a job well done is just as important as constructive criticism for sloppy or unsatisfactory work. Such praise is a way of reinforcing positive behavior.

1. *Objectives of evaluating*

   • to ensure that students continue to be productive and motivated throughout their work term

   • to provide students with the opportunity to learn and develop their capacities in and through the work experience

2. *Guidelines for Evaluating Performance*

   • Clearly inform students about the evaluation process
   During orientation students should be informed of any formal evaluations. This is a good time to remind them that student supervisors are often contacted for references by prospective employers.

   • Maintain privacy
   It is appropriate to praise in front of peers, but criticism should always be on an individual basis.

   • Be positive
   A note or memo commending good work is always in order. Some supervisors reward particular behavior with individual awards for being on time, for accuracy, or for giving exceptional service to a patron. Even when commenting on poor performance with a particular student, begin with the things the student does well, then discuss the problems.

   • Be specific
   Cite actual examples of satisfactory or unsatisfactory work, how often and when it occurred. By being specific, defensive responses from students with unsatisfactory work are minimized.

   • Be constructive
   Explore together ways to improve unsatisfactory performance. Ask for the student's suggestions, then make your own if necessary.

   • Be clear about your expectations and the results you are looking for.

Determine a plan for what is to be done by what date. If poor performance has already been discussed and there has been no improvement, the next meeting can be a dismissal warning. If a dismissal warning is given it should be in writing as well as verbal. *Figure 15* is a sample form of a dismissal warning.

- Comment on improved or deteriorating performance.
  Because errors often stand out, some supervisors tend to point out errors to the employee but forget to comment on good performance, taking it for granted. It is always a good idea to actively notice good performance, but it is especially important to do so when performance has improved after it was criticized. Conversely, some supervisors find it easier to praise than to criticize. Both praise and criticism offered in an objective, descriptive, nonpersonal way are important to the employee's professional development.

3. *Formal Evaluation*

The formal evaluation serves to set aside a time when both you and your student employee can think about and discuss not only overall performance but also future plans. In addition to conveying your evaluation, you should expect to hear ideas from the student employee about how the work is going as well as about changes that person would like to see implemented.

In preparing for the evaluation, here are some issues to consider:

- How to involve the student employee in the process
  Make an appointment with the student for the formal evaluation. Remind the student of the criteria you will be using for making judgments. Ask the student to come to the meeting prepared to give views on the same criteria and to propose any changes that would improve the work situation. Then, during the evaluation, invite the student to present these ideas before you present yours. Having the student employee go first enables you to get a quick reading on how similarly you both perceive the student's job and performance. Hopefully, there will be enough for you to agree with that you can start the evaluation on a positive note. It often happens that

you will give higher marks to the student than the student gave for the same performance. When criticizing performance, remember to be specific in describing the reasons for your judgments.

- When will the formal evaluation take place?
  About three months after hiring is a good time for a first formal evaluation. After that, it should be scheduled at least once a year.

- Who has access to the evaluation?
  Clarify this issue with the person in charge of personnel in your library.

Student employee evaluation forms usually list work behaviors and attributes and include some form of ranking scale. If such a form is used, all supervisors should agree on a common meaning of the scale. For example, will you rate employees on "how close" they are to the ideal, or how well they are progressing toward the ideal? *Figure 12* is a sample student employee evaluation form.

Apart from your meeting with individual student employees, you can learn a lot from conducting a survey among them to get a sense of how they perceive the library in general and work in your department in particular.

Figure 13 is a survey form we have used in the past. *Figure 14* presents a tally of the results of one such survey.

Figure 12

SAMPLE STUDENT EMPLOYEE EVALUATION FORM

Name _____ Date of hire _____

Job Title _____

List principal functions or duties of the student and rate them accordingly.

PRINCIPAL DUTIES   **RATING** (AND NOTES)

RATINGS: 1 = exceeds expectations; 2 = meets expectations; 3 = does not meet expectations

1. _____

2. _____

3. _____

4. _____

5. _____

ADDITIONAL WORK-RELATED FACTORS

	HIGH	AVERAGE	LOW
Initiative displayed:			
Dependability:			
Quality of work:			
Quantity of work:			
Patron interaction:			
Other:			

OVERALL EVALUATION

Employer's comments:

_____   _____

Student Employee's Signature   Date   Supervisor's Signature   Date

Figure 13

SAMPLE SURVEY OF STUDENT EMPLOYEES EXPECTATIONS / PERCEPTIONS

1. What have you liked most about working in the library?

2. What have you liked least about working in the library?

3. What benefits have you derived from working in the library?

Figure 14

SAMPLE RESULTS OF STUDENT EMPLOYEE SURVEY

1. MOST LIKED (out of 66 responses)

STAFF	26
ENVIRONMENT	21
HOURS	19
WORKING WITH PEOPLE	14
KNOWLEDGE OF THE LIBRARY	10

2. LEAST LIKED (out of 66 responses)

WORK IS BORING	19
SPECIFIC DUTIES	18
INTERFERES WITH STUDYING	8
RUDE CUSTOMERS	5
NOTHING	14

3. BENEFITS (out of 60 responses)

WORK WITH OTHERS/LEARN COOPERATION	36
PREPARATION FOR FUTURE	30
COMMUNICATION	23
LEARNED A LOT	20
MORE RESPONSIBILITY	19
SHARPENED SKILLS	19
UNDERSTANDING OTHERS	15
PATIENCE	8
SELF-DISCIPLINE	6
NICE SUPERVISORS	5

Figure 15

SAMPLE DISMISSAL WARNING

To:

From:

Subject: Warning

Date:

This is written notification that your dismissal is being considered for the following reason(s):

From now on, you are expected to improve your performance by doing the following:

_____   _____
Signature of Supervisor   *Date*

D. CASE STUDIES IN SUPERVISION

Following are some typical scenarios in the day of a student supervisor. They are designed to help you think about and discuss how to handle situations that commonly arise. Some questions have been provided to get you started.

If you are taking this workshop by yourself, think about alternative ways you might handle each case if you were the supervisor. Then, discuss your ideas with your supervisor or coworkers.

If you are taking this workshop as a participant in a class, break up into groups of three or four. Each group member should read the case example. Then, as a small group, discuss alternative ways of handling the situation imagining that you were the supervisor in the case. The small-group discussion should last one-half hour; then in plenary session, share the ideas your group came up with. If time is an issue, assign one, two, or three case studies to any one group, relying on the plenary discussion to familiarize everyone with all of the case studies.

Notice that the last case study is yours to fill in. Now is the time to look at your *Pre-workshop Exercise* sheet (Exercise 1), in which you identified a supervisory problem that concerns you.

1. THE NO-SHOW

Karen is a junior who has worked at the library for six months. She made plans to go away for the weekend when she was scheduled to work in the library. She was unable to find a substitute for her Saturday hours. She tried to contact her supervisor but was unable to reach him. Karen told a library co-worker to tell the supervisor and then went off for her weekend. The co-worker forgot to tell the supervisor; consequently no one showed up to work for those hours on Saturday.

What should be done?

Should Karen be fired?

Should the co-worker be reprimanded?

What, exactly, would you say?

2. *THE ELUSIVE PROBLEM-CREATOR*

Fourteen students work at the circulation desk. All of the students are to perform the same routine tasks and all have some guidelines to follow. As the year progresses it becomes evident that one or two of the students are not performing adequately. These students are not following the guidelines and policies. As supervisor, you have not been able to identify who the lax students are. You do, however, see the results.

Should you ignore the situation?

If you take action, how can the situation be corrected without making all the students feel guilty?

3. *THE GOOD WORKER GONE BAD*

John has worked in the library for over a year. He is a good worker, always completing tasks accurately and on time. Lately, you suspect he is being dishonest about work hours. You notice that John is reading the paper or doing his homework without punching out his time card. The time cards are located in another area so it is difficult to confirm these suspicions.

Should you ignore the situation?

Should you confront John? If so, how?

4. FRIENDS WHO COME CALLING

Ann is a very hard working student in the cataloging department. She is well liked by all her co-workers. Her friends often stop in to visit while she is working. Even though Ann continues her work, the talking and laughing disturb the other staff members in the area. Ann doesn't seem to notice that she and her friends are causing a disruption of others' work.

Should you talk to Ann?

Should you talk to Ann's friends?

What, exactly, would you say?

5. POOR WORK HABITS

Don is a new student to the library, working in circulation. You are concerned that he always shows up for work late. A few times he has not come to work at all and has provided no substitutes. This means you must take over Don's task or ask another student to stay for a longer period of time. Recently other students have complained to you about Don's work habits. From your standpoint, Don seems to convey that he is not expected to take the work seriously; he will get his work award anyway.

Should Don be fired immediately? Given another chance?

6. A CO-SUPERVISOR ISN'T AS GOOD AS YOU

Pat is a friend of yours who has worked for you in the past. This year she is again working in the library but has been assigned to another department under the supervision of another staff member. After a few weeks, while you are talking to Pat, she indicates she is very uncomfortable with the new job. Pat tells you that she has had very little training and is unsure about what to do on the job.

Should you train Pat yourself?

Should you approach Pat's current supervisor and relate what you were told?

What would you do next?

7. YOU INHERIT A BAD SITUATION

You are the new supervisor of a department in which there is a staff member who has worked in your library for many years. She has a longer tenure that anyone else and has become a "fixture." As the only full-time staff member besides yourself, she is in charge of student workers. She does not like to work with student workers, has a tendency to make the students nervous, and is at times unfriendly.

Do you explain this to students you are assigning to work with her? If so, how?

Do you say nothing?

What can you do about the "fixture"?

8. THE SLOW WORKER

Melinda's work is accurate and in every way high quality, but she is extremely slow.

Would you ignore it?

If not, how would you handle it?

9. THE SMELLY WORKER

Charlie is a conscientious worker, but he smells of body odor. His co-workers at the circulation desk have complained to you that they cannot work side-by-side with him.

Do you tell the co-workers they have to put up with it?

Do you raise the issue with Charlie? If so, how?

9. THE FAST WORKER

Bernard's work is extremely fast and accurate, so he usually finishes his assignments before his hours are up and spends the rest of the time chatting with co-workers or doing his homework.

Would you give him more work to do?

Ask him to stop interrupting co-workers but allow the homework?

Ask him to leave early when his work is done, thereby saving you money?

Look the other way because he is such a good worker.

11. *YOUR STUDENT EMPLOYEE PROBLEM*
Refer to your notes in Exercise 1.

E. SUMMARY OF MODULE 4

Key ideas I learned about supervising:

CONCLUSION

You now have an overview of principles governing effective management of student employees and techniques to apply those principles.

Now is a good time to review your annotations on the following sheets:

Page xi: Pre-workshop Exercise
Page   8: Summary of Module 1:   The Nature of Student Employment
Page 20: Summary of Module 2:   Hiring the Right Person
Page 34: Summary of Module 3:   Training
Page 50: Summary of Module 4:   Supervising and Evaluating

We hope that what you have learned in this workshop will increase your effectiveness as a manager of student library employees.

APPENDICES

APPENDIX 1: PRESENTATION SLIDES

1. Title
2. Agenda
3. Facts About Student Employees
4. What's Special About Student Employees
5. Peripheral Workers
6. External Motivators
7. How to Create External Motivators
8. Job Description: Contents
9. Purpose of the Interview
10. Conducting the Interview
11. Orientation: The Big Picture
12. Orientation: Departmental
13. Supervisor as Trainer
14. The Written Training Plan
15. The Training Session
16. Giving Criticism and Praise During Training
17. Functions of a Student Supervisor
18. Supervisory Styles
19. The Supportive Supervisor
20. Build External Motivators Into Job Description
21. Functions of Performance Appraisal
22. Guidelines for Evaluating
23. The Formal Evaluation

Managing
Student
Library
Employees

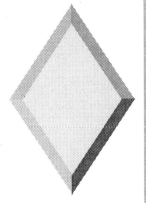

Agenda

- **The Nature of Student Employment**

- **Hiring the Right Person**

- **Training**

- **Supervising**

- **Evaluating**

Facts About Student Employees

- ◆ Major component of staff
- ◆ Cost-saver for library
- ◆ Lowest in hierarchy
- ◆ Require disproportionate efforts to manage

What's Special About Student Employees?

- ◆ Excellent pool of part-time workers to fill library's part-time needs
  - a. long hours of operation
  - b. brief stints
  - c. special skills but not full-time
- ◆ Handle the library's routine work so other staff can do the complex work

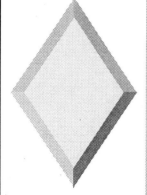

Peripheral Workers

- Have partial commitment to the organization

- View work as job, not career

- Regard job as secondary to other activities

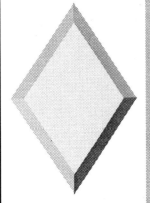

External Motivators

- Clear job requirements
- Job is valued by organization
- Consistent, fair application of rules
- Job includes taking responsibility and being accountable
- Assurance of continued learning
- Good performance is acknowledged

How to Create External Motivators

- ◆ Clarify job expectations
- ◆ Demonstrate importance of job
- ◆ Ensure unbiased treatment of all staff
- ◆ Assign responsibility
- ◆ Hold employee accountable
- ◆ Recognize accomplishments
- ◆ Support continual learning
- ◆ Reward high-quality work

Job Description: Contents

- Components of the job
- Skills, knowledge required
- Skills, knowledge desired
- Work schedule requirements
- Workload expectations

Purpose of the Interview

- Gain information to supplement application
- Find fit between supervisor, employee, job
- Begin building external motivators
  - by communicating
  - a. importance of job
  - b. your expectations

Conducting the Interview

HIRING

- ◆ Relate questions to job components
- ◆ Relate questions to desired skills
- ◆ Formulate questions that elicit past experiences
- ◆ Choose words carefully

HIRING

Orientation:
The Big Picture

- Sets tone, attitudes
- Provides general information about library
- Conveys importance and accomplishments of library
- Includes why job and employee are important
- Articulates library's mission
- Covers employment policies and procedures
- Introduces other staff

Orientation: Departmental

HIRING

- Covers departmental goals

- Describes role of department within library

- Highlights major departmental issues, policies

- Introduces other staff in unit

Supervisor as Trainer

- Starts good working relationships
- Should know job well
- Knows what works better or worse
- Sets expectations
- Begins communication pattern

The Written Training Plan

HIRING

- No best format
- Serves as guide
- Helps decide order of training
- Makes clear what's left
- Is an external motivator

HIRING

The Training Session

- Two-way process
- Should include supplementary materials
- Should be tested

HIRING

Giving Criticism and Praise During Training

- ◆ Regard mistakes as opportunities to clarify

- ◆ Praise correct behavior

- ◆ Address right and wrong close to when they are done

- ◆ Be specific in describing what you observe or feel

- ◆ Never accuse or blame

- ◆ Never ascribe motives or attribute attitude

Functions of a Student Supervisor

- ◆ Clarify the nature of tasks
- ◆ Reduce roadblocks
- ◆ Monitor continuing performance
- ◆ Be a go-between

Supervisory Styles

SUPERVISING

- ◆ Directive
- ◆ Participative
- ◆ Achievement-oriented
- ◆ Supportive

The Supportive Supervisor

SUPERVISING

- ◆ Clarifies nature of the work
- ◆ Gives responsibility
- ◆ Relates student's skills learned to future career

Build External Motivators
Into Job Design

SUPERVISING

- ◆ Require diversity of skills to be used

- ◆ Organize work so it can be accomplished in defined intervals and quantities

- ◆ Impact of work should be explicit

- ◆ Allow discretion and control

- ◆ Reinforce expectations through frequent feedback

EVALUATING

Functions of Performance Appraisal

- Provides important feedback to employee

- Tool for communicating

- Mechanism for setting new goals

- Ensures continuous productivity

- Means of developing new areas for learning

Guidelines for Evaluating

EVALUATING

- ◆ Inform employee of the process
- ◆ Maintain privacy
- ◆ Be positive
- ◆ Be specific
- ◆ Be constructive
- ◆ Be clear about expectations and results
- ◆ Comment on improved or deteriorating performance

EVALUATING

The Formal Evaluation

- ◆ Involve student employee in the process

- ◆ Timing: 3 months after hiring, then annually

- ◆ Clarify who has access to evaluation

- ◆ Forms: all supervisors should agree on meaning of rankings

- ◆ Conduct occasional survey

APPENDIX 2: REFERENCES

1. Association of Research Libraries. ARL Statistics. Washington, DC: Association of Research Libraries, 1992, page 30.

2. Childress, Schelley H. "Training of Student Assistants in College Libraries: Some Insights and Ideas." *Arkansas Libraries* 44 (1987): 25-27.

3. Christenson, John, Larry Benson and Julene Butler. "An Evaluation of Reference Desk Service." *College and Research Library News* (1989):468-83.

4. Cottam, Keith M. "An Experience with Student Assistance." *Utah Libraries* 12 (Fall 1969): 24-27.

5. Crawford, Gregory A. "Training Student Employees by Videotape." *College and Research Library News* 49 (March 1988): 149-50.

6. Dawkins, Willie Mae, and Jeffrey Jackson. "Enhancing Reference Services: Students as Assistants." *Technicalities* 6 (1986): 4-7.

7. Demus, Samuel. "On Library Student Assistants." *Cornell University Library Bulletin* 209 (July 1978): 14-17.

8. Dougherty, Richard M., and Fred J. Heinritz. *Scientific Management of Library Operations.* 2nd ed. New Jersey: The Scarecrow Press, 1982.

9. Dubrin, Andrew J. *Leadership: Research, Findings, Practice, and Skills.* New York: Houghton Mifflin Co., 1995, 122–30.

10. Evered, James. "How to Write a Good Job Description." *Supervisory Management* (April 1981):17.

11. Faller, Martha Lewkus. "Training Student Workers in Community College Libraries: The Importance of a Handbook." *Junior College Libraries* 1 (Fall 1982): 57-64.

12. Folmsbee, Mark Alan, and James W. Quinn. "Circulation Management, Desk Attendants and Limited Resources: A Challenge and an Opportunity for the New Circulation Librarian." *Legal Reference Services Quarterly* 8 (1988): 245-52.

13. Ford, Robert N. *Motivation Through the Work Itself.* New York: Amacom, 1969.

14. Frank, Donald G. "Management of Student Assistants in a Public Services Setting of an Academic Library." *RQ* 24 (Fall 1984): 51-57.

15. Fuller, F. Jay. "Employing Library Student Assistants as Student Supervisors." *College and Research Libraries News* 51 (October 1990): 855-57.

16 Fuller, F. Jay. "A Student Assistant Program for the Nineties." *College and Research Libraries News* 48 (December 1987): 688-92.

17. Gaines, James Edwin, Jr. "The Student Assistant in Academic Libraries: A Study of Personnel Administration Practices and Constraints." (Ph.D. dissertation, Florida State University, 1977).

18. Gannon, Martin J. "The Management of Peripheral Employees." *Personnel Journal* 56 (February 1976): 68-71+.

19. Guilfoyle, Marvin. "Computer Assisted Training for Student Library Assistants." *Journal of Academic Librarianship* 10 (January 1985): 333-36.

20. Hackman, J.R., and G.R. Oldham. "Motivation Through the Design of Work: Test of a Theory." *Organizational Behavior and Human Performance* 16 (1976): 256.

21. Heinlen, William F. "Using Student Assistants in Academic Reference." *RQ* 5 (Summer 1976): 323-25.

22. Herzberg, Fredrick B. Mausner, and B. Snyderman. *The Motivation to Work* New York: John Wiley and Sons, 1959.

23. Hodge, Stanley P. "Performance Appraisals: Developing a Sound Legal and Managerial System." *College and Research Libraries* 44 (July 1983): 240.

24. House, Robert J. "Let's Not Forget About New Employee Orientation." *Personnel Journal* 57 (February 1976): 245-46.

25. House, Robert J. and Terrence R. Mitchell. "Path-Goal Theory of Leadership," *Journal of Contemporary Business* (Autumn 1994): 81-98.

26. Joyce, Mary Ann. "Developing and Negotiating Job Standards." *The Bookmark* (Summer 1982): 213.

27. Kathman, Michael and Sherman Hayes. "The College Library as Guinea Pig: Student Projects in the Library. *College and Research Libraries News* 53;9 (October 1992): 572-74.

28. Kathman, Michael D. and Jane M. Kathman. "Integrating Student Employees into the Management Structure of Academic Libraries." *Catholic Library World* (March 1985): 328-30.

29. ———. "Management Problems of Student Workers in Academic Libraries." *College and Research Libraries* 39 (March 1978): 118-22.

30. ———. Managing Student Workers in College Libraries (CLIP Note No. 7). Association of College and Research Libraries, 1986.

31.   ———. "Performance Measures for Student Assistants." *College and Research Libraries* 53;4 (July 1992): 299-304.

32.   ———. "Student Employee Training," In *Improving Teaching and Training in Libraries* edited by Trish Ridgewa. AMS Press, 1993.

33.   ———, comps. Managing Student Employees in College Libraries (CLIP Note No. 20). Association of College and Research Libraries, 1994, page 20.

34.   Kendrick, Curtis L. "Cavalry to the Rescue: The Use of Temporary Employees in the Place of Student Assistants." *College and Research Library News* 50 (April 1989): 273-74.

35.   Lyons, Evelyn. "Student Workers in the College Library." In *Operations Handbook for the Small Academic Library,* edited by Gerald B. McCabe, 91-8. New York: Greenwood Press, 1989.

36.   MacAdam, Barbara and Darlene P. Nichols. "Peer Information Counseling at the University of Michigan Undergraduate Library." *Journal of Academic Librarianship* 36 (May 1988): 80-81.

37.   McCarthy, Constance. "Paraprofessionals, Student Assistants, and the Reference Clan: an Application of Contemporary Management Theory. In *Academic Libraries: Myths and Realities,* edited by Suzanne Dodson,382-86. Seattle: Association of College and Research Libraries, 1984.

38.   McGlelland, David C. *Human Motivation.* Glenview, IL: Scott Foresman, 1985.

39.   Melnyk, Andrew. "Student Aides in our Library (Blessings and Headaches)." *Illinois Library* 58 (Fall 1976): 141-44.

40.   Mintzberg, Henry. *The Nature of Managerial Work* New York: Harper and Row, 1970.

41.   Morris, Betty J. "Student Assistants in Academic Libraries: A Study of Training Practices." (Ph.D. dissertation, University of Alabama, 1984).

42.   Morse, Dean. *The Peripheral Worker.* New York: Columbia University Press, 1969.

43.   Payne, Sherry. "Management of Student Assistants." *West Virginia Library* 31 (Winter 1978): 22-23.

44.   Rao, Dittakavi Nagasankara. "Student Assistants in Libraries." *Herald of Library Science* 23 (January-April 1984): 3-6.

45.   Rawlins, Susan M. "Technology and the Personal Touch: Computer-Assisted Instruction for Library Student Workers." *Journal of Academic Librarianship* 8 (1982): 26-29.

46.   Repp, Joan and Julia A. Woods. "Student Appraisal Study and Allocation Formula: Priorities & Equitable Funding in a University." *Journal of Academic Librarianship* 6 (May 1980): 87-90.

47. Richter, Anita T. "Student Assistants in the Library." *Catholic Library World* (1978): 391-94.

48. Roark, Mary L. "Work on the Campus: Benefits for Student and Institution." ED 235443.

49. Robertson, Ellen and Carol Krismann. "Using Student Assistant Resources to Solve a Problem Creatively." *Colorado Library* 13 (September 1987): 25.

50. Shabel, Donald. "Performance Standards and Cost Analysis." *Illinois Librarians* 64 (Spring 1982): 875.

51. Sichel, Beatrice. "Utilizing Student Assistants in Small Libraries." *Journal of Library Administration* 13 (Spring 1982): 35-45.

52. Smith, Nathan M. "For Student Assistants - Programmed Training." *Utah Libraries* 14 (Fall 1971): 13-15.

53. Smith, Robert F. and Kerry Tucker. "Measuring Individual Performance." *Public Relations Journal* 38 (October 1982): 27.

54. Steers, Richard M., and Lyman W. Porter, eds.. *Motivation and Work Behavior,* 3rd edition, New York: McGraw-Hill, 1983.

55. Tabbetts, Daine R., and Hugh Pritchard. "Undergraduate Aids." *RQ* 12 (1973): 275-76.

56. Vocino, Michael and Martha H. Kellog. "Student Employees in Academic Libraries: Premise and Potential." ED 301220.

57. Westbrook, Lynn. "Students and Support Staff on the Reference Desk (at the Undergraduate Library, University of Michigan)." *College and Research Library News* 9 (October 1989): 808+.

58. White, Emilie C. "Student Assistants in Academic Libraries: From Reluctance to Reliance." *Journal of Academic Librarianship* 11 (May 1985): 93-97.

59. Woodward, Beth S. "Effectiveness of an Information Desk Staffed by Graduate Students and Nonprofessionals." *College and Research Library News* 50 (July 1989): 455-67.

60. Young, Arthur P. "Student Assistants: A Report and a Challenge." *RQ* 9 (Summer 1970): 296-97.

APPENDIX 3: TRAINER'S AIDS

This section contains:

Presentation Slides (miniatures for handout)

Notes to the Trainer

PRESENTATION SLIDES

Managing Student Library Employees

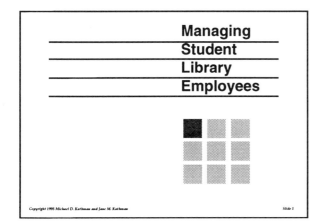

Slide 1

 ## Agenda

- The Nature of Student Employment
- Hiring the Right Person
- Training
- Supervising
- Evaluating

Slide 2

 ## Facts About Student Employees

- Major component of staff
- Cost-saver for library
- Lowest in hierarchy
- Require disproportionate efforts to manage

Slide 3

 ## What's Special About Student Employees?

- Excellent pool of part-time workers to fill library's part-time needs
    - a. long hours of operation
    - b. brief stints
    - c. special skills but not full-time
- Handle the library's routine work so other staff can do the complex work

Slide 4

 ## Peripheral Workers

- Have partial commitment to the organization
- View work as job, not career
- Regard job as secondary to other activities

Slide 5

 ## External Motivators

- Clear job requirements
- Job is valued by organization
- Consistent, fair application of rules
- Job includes taking responsibility and being accountable
- Assurance of continued learning
- Good performance is acknowledged

Slide 6

How to Create External Motivators

- Clarify job expectations
- Demonstrate importance of job
- Ensure unbiased treatment of all staff
- Assign responsibility
- Hold employee accountable
- Recognize accomplishments
- Support continual learning
- Reward high-quality work

Slide 7

Job Description: Contents

- Components of the job
- Skills, knowledge required
- Skills, knowledge desired
- Work schedule requirements
- Workload expectations

Slide 8

Purpose of the Interview

- Gain information to supplement application
- Find fit between supervisor, employee, job
- Begin building external motivators
  by communicating
  a. importance of job
  b. your expectations

Slide 9

Conducting the Interview

- Relate questions to job components
- Relate questions to desired skills
- Formulate questions that elicit past experiences
- Choose words carefully

Slide 10

Orientation: The Big Picture

- Sets tone, attitudes
- Provides general information about library
- Conveys importance and accomplishments of library
- Includes why job and employee are important
- Articulates library's mission
- Covers employment policies and procedures
- Introduces other staff

Slide 11

Orientation: Departmental

- Covers departmental goals
- Describes role of department within library
- Highlights major departmental issues, policies
- Introduces other staff in unit

Slide 12

Supervisor as Trainer

- Starts good working relationships
- Should know job well
- Knows what works better or worse
- Sets expectations
- Begins communication pattern

 The Written Training Plan

- No best format
- Serves as guide
- Helps decide order of training
- Makes clear what's left
- Is an external motivator

 The Training Session

- Two-way process
- Should include supplementary materials
- Should be tested

 Giving Criticism and Praise During Training

- Regard mistakes as opportunities to clarify
- Praise correct behavior
- Address right and wrong close to when they are done
- Be specific in describing what you observe or feel
- Never accuse or blame
- Never ascribe motives or attribute attitude

 Functions of a Student Supervisor

- Clarify the nature of tasks
- Reduce roadblocks
- Monitor continuing performance
- Be a go-between

 Supervisory Styles

- Directive
- Participative
- Achievement-oriented
- Supportive

SUPERVISING

The Supportive Supervisor

- Clarifies nature of the work
- Gives responsibility
- Relates student's skills learned to future career

 SUPERVISING

Build External Motivators Into Job Design

- Require diversity of skills to be used
- Organize work so it can be accomplished in defined intervals and quantities
- Impact of work should be explicit
- Allow discretion and control
- Reinforce expectations through frequent feedback

 EVALUATING

Functions of Performance Appraisal

- Provides important feedback to employee
- Tool for communicating
- Mechanism for setting new goals
- Ensures continuous productivity
- Means of developing new areas for learning

 EVALUATING

Guidelines for Evaluating

- Inform employee of the process
- Maintain privacy
- Be positive
- Be specific
- Be constructive
- Be clear about expectations and results
- Comment on improved or deteriorating performance

EVALUATING

The Formal Evaluation

- Involve student employee in the process
- Timing: 3 months after hiring, then annually
- Clarify who has access to evaluation
- Forms: all supervisors should agree on meaning of rankings
- Conduct occasional survey

NOTES TO THE TRAINER

This workshop is designed so that the reader can work through the four modules and exercises alone. However, we feel that an individual can have a richer experience taking this workshop in a group, under the guidance of a trainer or facilitator who underscores key points, responds to questions, and moderates discussion. For the group trainer, here are some suggestions:

1. *Length of session*

    Decide how much time you and your class will spend on this workshop, and then divide up the time among one or more of the four modules. It is possible to do all four modules in a full day (9:00am-noon; 1:00pm-4:30pm), but you would have to be selective in what you cover from each one, and sacrifice quality interaction between you and the participants and among the participants themselves. We have had as much success teaching one module at a time over an extended period of time as we have had teaching the whole workshop over one and one-half days.

2. *Size of group*

    Try to keep the group to 20–30 people. Remember, the larger the group, the less time there will be to deal with individual participants' issues. Forty participants is about as large a group as you would want. With so large a group, your interaction with participants on an individual basis will be limited; but if you structure the exercises so that the break-out groups are small enough (three to four in a group), participants will be able to air at least some of their concerns and receive a fair amount of feedback from fellow participants.

3. *Diversity of participants*

    If you are training staff who work in a single institution, you are in the excellent position of being able to arrange follow-up sessions and consultations. This should result in a critical mass of supervisors having a common background of knowledge and skills, so that progress should be quite noticeable librarywide relatively soon after the workshop. If your audience comes from diverse institutions, use their differences to enrich everyone's knowledge by encouraging discussion about their varied experiences.

4. *Change takes time*

Remind participants that change won't happen overnight. The size of the department or library, the degree of complexity of operations, the relative longevity of staff, the magnitude of the change they are hoping to achieve—all of these are factors affecting how long it will take for real change to occur. Urge participants to work on achieving changes piecemeal—one issue or problem at a time.

5. *Advance preparation*

When you confirm advance registrations, ask enrollees to bring to the workshop a job description for a student employee they supervise. They will make use of it several times throughout the workshop.

If you like, you may also send them the Pre-workshop Exercise (page xi) to fill out and bring with them to the workshop. It will give them a head start in thinking about their reasons for attending the workshop.

Make arrangements for a room that is the right size and appropriately furnished. Tables for four or six work well. They should be arranged so that the participants face the instructor's station.

For equipment, you will need an overhead projector and screen (and, if you are using the diskettes provided with the PLUS edition of this book, a microcomputer and projection panel) and an easel with a newsprint pad and marking pens. Include masking tape to hang newsprint pages on wall—but first be sure you have permission to tape things to the walls in your training room.

6. *The day of the workshop*

Arrive early and check out the room arrangement and equipment. Try viewing an overhead slide from the seats in the far back and extremities of the room. Move furniture till you are sure all seats in the house are good. (If you are training in an unfamiliar facility, it is wise to put everything you are expecting that facility to provide in writing beforehand. You might even draw a picture of the room arrangement that works best for you.)

Have handouts ready. If you want to encourage people to sit in the front row seats, distribute the handouts in advance of the session. Place one on each chair.

If it is likely that most participants do not know each other, have name tags ready.

Have blank paper available for participants to use for taking notes and doing exercises.

Project the title slide onto the screen while the participants gather— as a point of reference for those entering the room.

While participants wait for the session to begin, have those who have not done so complete the Pre-Workshop Exercise (p. xi). Remember, it gets them thinking about problems they would like to have covered in the workshop, and they will use the sheet for making special notes throughout the session. They can also refer to it when doing the case studies exercise in Module 4.

7. *Your opening remarks*

Introduce yourself and, if participants are strangers to each other, ask each to say their name and library.

8. *Exercises*

Before each exercise, review the instructions to be sure everyone has a common understanding about what is expected. Indicate how much time they will have to do the exercise.

When doing the case studies (pp.45-49), be sure to tell participants that they are free to work on their own situation (p.50). In our experience, many participants believe that this opportunity to grapple with their own problem is the point at which the workshop came together for them. Remind those who so wish to refer to the concerns they noted in the Pre-Workshop Exercise.

9. *Don't try to cover everything*

If you find that your timing is off and you have spent more time than you had planned on one segment, don't try to cover all the rest by speeding up. Nor should you drop an entire segment. Instead, cover the more major points in each segment and encourage participants to delve deeper or work on other parts of the topic on their own.

This is especially practical when each participant has a copy of this book as a handout.

10. *Closing*

End the session by summarizing what you have covered, highlighting key points you want them to remember.

APPENDIX 4: SAMPLE STUDENT EMPLOYEE ORIENTATION HANDBOOKS

This section contains:

Sample student employee handbook from a small college library

Sample student employee handbook from a large university special services department

Sample student employee handbook from a large university branch library

These materials have been reproduced with permission.

SAMPLE STUDENT EMPLOYEE HANDBOOK FROM A SMALL COLLEGE LIBRARY

WELCOME TO THE LIBRARY

Welcome to the Library. We are pleased you have join our staff for the coming year. Your position as a student employee will require you to learn a great many things in a short time. The work that you do is a necessary part of library service - the library would have great difficulty meeting its service needs without you.

By working with us you should learn not only the job you do for the library, but also how to use the library more effectively for your own studies.

We are a service organization and expect everyone on the staff to be courteous and friendly toward those who use our services. Remember, the library can be threatening for some people. Your helpful presence can make the library a help rather than a hindrance for your colleagues.

As a user as well as a provider of Library Services, you are in a unique position to help us improve our services. Please feel free to contact me or any of the staff when you have suggestions or comments. Together we can continue a strong tradition of service.

Director of Libraries

MISSION STATEMENT

The Library is dedicated to providing resources and services that will stimulate intellectual curiosity and facilitate learning and research within the academic community. We are committed to carrying out these responsibilities in a manner that is consistent with the liberal arts character of our institution. In providing library services, we are also aware that the information environment of the present day is far more complex than in times past and that this complexity requires the services of a staff which is deeply committed to assisting library users as they seek the information they need. Even though the library now makes resources available that would have been undreamed of a decade or two ago, it is the services of the libraries which make these resources accessible.

WORK SCHEDULES

You will be able to schedule the number of hours necessary to meet your work award. You are responsible for these hours. If you are unable to work your scheduled hours, for whatever reason, it is your responsibility to find a substitute. Failure to report for work without finding a substitute will result in termination. If you are substituting for another student, you are responsible for the shift. Please be prompt in reporting for duty and do not leave until a replacement shows up. A list of student workers and their phone numbers has been given to you. Make sure to report all schedule changes to your supervisor.

TIME CARDS

You are required to punch in and out every time you report for work using the time cards and clock located at the Circulation Desk. When punching in and out, please make certain all times are legible. Record the hours and minutes you have worked on your daily time card in the box beneath the punched time. Your time cards are due in the Financial Aid Office on the 22nd of each month. Approximately 1 week before the time cards are due you will find a computer time card with your name on it located near the time clock. Please sign the card where it says "Student Signature". Your time will be transferred from your yellow time card to the computer cards, totaled, and signed by your supervisor. The area supervisor will also make certain the time cards are brought to the Financial Aid Office. If you fail to sign a computer time card you will not be paid. Should you forget to punch in or out, have your supervisor write in and initial the time.

WORK HABITS

All persons entering the library are our patrons be they students, instructors, staff members, or people from the community. Your job is a very important part of the service we give our patrons. Train yourself to smile, be tactful, speak softly, and have a pleasant manner.

Your immediate supervisor will train you in the skills needed in the area where you are working. It is important that you learn your job thoroughly. Do not be afraid to ask questions when you are in doubt or do not know something. Your supervisor expects you to ask questions.

You are not expected to be an expert at answering reference questions; therefore, please direct all reference questions to the Reference Librarian. You may assist library patrons in locating materials when asked for assistance; however, you should feel free to ask for assistance if you are unsure of where the material is or if you feel the patron may need more help than just knowing where the "Q's" are located. Under no circumstances should you tell a patron we have no information on a subject or that we do not have a particular book - refer all such problems to the reference librarian.

The smooth running of the library depends on your being dependable and punctual. Your co-workers and our patrons are depending on you.

Avoid long conversations with friends and fellow workers. Not only does this interfere with your work but it also interrupts the concentration of those studying.

Do not eat, drink, or smoke on the job. When all work is completed please check with your supervisor for further assignments.

Walkmans are not to be used in any job where you have or might have contact with the public. For student employees not dealing directly with the public, the use of Walkmans is up to the discretion of the immediate supervisor.

While you are on the job your personal appearance and habits reflect not only on you but also on the library as well. In appearance and habits you should be neat, clean, and wear clothing suitable to a business-like atmosphere.

TELEPHONES

The library telephones are for library business. If it is necessary that you use the telephone, limit your call to a few minutes. You should not receive personal calls at work unless it is an emergency.

EVALUATIONS

Your performance will be evaluated by your immediate supervisor on an annual basis. These evaluations are not only used by the Financial Aid Office in determining work eligibility for the next year, they are also used by prospective employers upon graduation. One copy of the evaluation form is kept in your files in the library and one copy is kept in the Financial Aid Office.

TERMINATION

If your job performance proves unsatisfactory you will be issued a verbal warning and, if improvement is not made, a written warning. If no improvement is shown within the time frame set in the written warning (usually two weeks) your position here will be terminated. Remember that failure to report for work without finding a substitute will result in termination. Every effort will be made to resolve conflicts and continue your employment. If you are terminated from the Library, the University does not have to place you in another student employment position. Should you wish to terminate your employment, two weeks notice must be given to your supervisor and the Financial Aid Office.

_____

I have read this manual and understand what is expected of me as a student employee in the Library.

_____   _____
Your Signature   Your Supervisor's Signature

*From the Tarrant County Junior College Library's Manual
as adapted by St. John's University Library*

Cartoons by Clinton Crowley

SAMPLE STUDENT EMPLOYEE HANDBOOK FROM A LARGE UNIVERSITY SPECIAL SERVICES DEPARTMENT

This handbook was written by the then-head of the department, Suzanne Gallup Calpestri. To save space in this book, the text has been rearranged from its original 5.5" x 8.5" pamphlet form to its present, much denser appearance. Also, the cover and table of contents have been deleted. In the original format, those features of smaller size and uncluttered layout contributed to making the booklet very attractive and readable.

STUDENT EMPLOYEE HANDBOOK
COOPERATIVE SERVICES, THE LIBRARY, UNIVERSITY OF CALIFORNIA, BERKELEY

WELCOME
Welcome to the Cooperative Services Department. We are pleased to have you join our team. As part of the Public Service section of the Library we are here to make sure that students and faculty are successful in pursuing their research needs using the UC Berkeley Library system. In Cooperative Services, we assist in the information gathering process by providing document delivery services for our own collections and for collections throughout the world. We get the documents (e.g. reports, books, articles,etc.) that faculty, staff and students need whether or not we own the material.

We provide on-the-job training some of which may be beneficial to you as you use the libraries to pursue your own coursework. You will also get work experience in a service profession.

Once again, we're glad to have you join us. I look forward to meeting you when I visit your unit.

PURPOSE OF THIS HANDBOOK
As part of your general introduction to the Library you should have a copy of the Memorandum to Student Library Employees issued by the Library's Human Resources Dept. This memorandum outlines policies and procedures affecting student employment throughout the Library.

The purpose of the Cooperative Services Handbook is to amplify some sections of that memorandum and clarify Library Public Service policies in the context of your job. We think you'll be more successful on the job if you know in advance what we expect of you.

We hope this handbook will assist you in fulfilling your public service responsibilities.

ORGANIZATION OF COOPERATIVE SERVICES WITHIN PUBLIC SERVICES

Cooperative Services consists of three individual units: BAKER Service, Interlibrary Borrowing Service (IBS) and Interlibrary Lending Service (ILL). The units work together to provide document delivery services to the campus community and researchers worldwide.

WHO DOES WHAT

The BAKER Service delivers materials from UC Berkeley's libraries and libraries around the world to campus clientele, primarily faculty, graduate students and staff.

Interlibrary Borrowing Service arranges for loans and photocopies of materials not owned by UCB Libraries.

Interlibrary Lending Service is responsible for providing non- UCB users with access to UCB's collections either by loan or copy.

PUBLIC SERVICE IN THE LIBRARY: GOALS FOR COOPERATIVE SERVICES

Patron Satisfaction is our Business

The three units share several goals in common. First, it is important to deliver the correct material. This requires attention to detail and accuracy in performance of the job. A second goal is getting the material to the patron in time for it to be useful. This means meeting daily deadlines. A third goal is to provide a consistent level of service so that patrons know what they can expect when they use our services. This requires teamwork and is essential if patrons are to have confidence in the service we offer.

Finally, our interactions with the public should be courteous. This means we expect patrons to leave feeling that we have been helpful in moving them closer to their research goals even if we could not provide what they asked for initially. This is a tall order.

GUIDELINES AND PERFORMANCE STANDARDS FOR STUDENT EMPLOYEES

Although we are somewhat informal in our dealings with each other, office conduct is meant to be businesslike. Our office spaces are cramped and the volume of business is generally brisk. Each person's conduct has a direct impact on others in the room and on the end product. First and foremost, we are here to get a job done.

In general, talking and visiting while in the office is likely to interfere with the work of others. When speaking to others keep your voice low.

As a rule we expect you to maintain your work space as a place where library business is conducted and take care of personal matters during non-working hours. Please advise visitors or callers to reach you at work only in the event of an emergency, or special circumstance.

PUBLIC SERVICE CONDUCT

Some offices are public service areas (IBS and to a limited extent BAKER). Special attention to office decorum is essential in these work areas as it reflects on our public service image.

Eating and drinking is not permitted in public service areas as it conveys an unprofessional image of our work to the public. Sound equipment (radios, cassette players, etc.) may not be used in public service areas in the library.

WHEN YOU'RE NOT SURE, ASK

You will be trained to do the assignments required of you on this job. If you are asked to do something for which you have not been trained, be sure and speak up.

If you are unsure of any procedure, ask your supervisor for help. We can train better if we know what your questions are.

We will be mindful not to assign you to answer questions for which you have not been trained. However, if a patron asks you a question which goes beyond your training and expertise, please refer the patron to a career staff member. As a general rule if you think the answer to a patron's question is "NO" (we don't have that/we don't provide that service) you should refer the patron to a career staff member.

CARE FOR LIBRARY MATERIALS

The Library spends a lot of money each year repairing damaged library materials. It is essential that all staff handle library materials with care. In particular,
- xerox with caution;
- do not eat or drink near library materials;
- if you are working with a book which is fragile and may not withstand the processing in which you are engaged, talk with your supervisor before pro ceeding.

Your supervisor will apprise you of the conservation issues related to your job.

WORK SCHEDULES

In general, work assignments are made with two factors in mind:
1. Library deadlines, and
2. your class schedule. Students are normally assigned 12 - 15 hours per week. Students may not work more than 19 hours nor less than 10 hours per week on a regular basis.

In order for us to provide efficient service and to meet our goals for turnaround time, we depend on all student employees to adhere to a fixed schedule. Only agree to a schedule if you can maintain it throughout the semester.

Library services continue and are usually in very high demand during midterms and finals week. During midterms we may be able to adjust your regular schedule. We generally cannot eliminate you from the schedule so you can take the week off. Special schedules are arranged for finals week and intersession.

ABSENCES/TARDINESS

Although we expect employees to maintain dependable schedules, we recognize that there are times when employees need to be late to work, need to schedule time off from work, or are unable to work due to illness or some other unforeseen event.

Your supervisor will inform you of the unit procedures for tardiness, illness, modified work schedules, substitutions, etc.

WORK SHIFTS

Work shifts are generally for 2 hrs or more at a time. Students may not work 5 consecutive hours without punching out for at least 30 minutes. Students may not work more than 8 hours in one day.

BREAKS

Fifteen minute breaks with pay are scheduled at the convenience of the department for students working 3 or more consecutive hours. Before taking a break check with your supervisor to make sure that the time you have chosen is convenient to the unit.

As a rule breaks are to be taken outside the office. There is a staff room on the 4th floor equipped with vending machines and a microwave oven,etc.

Breaks cannot be accumulated or used for other purposes such as leaving early or adjusting work schedules. Breaks of more than 15 minutes, e.g. lunch breaks, are without pay. You must clock out for these times.

TIMECARDS

Timecards reflect time you are being paid to work. You are responsible for punching in when you arrive and out as you leave. If you should forget to punch in or out, or if you need to have corrections made to your timecard, please see your supervisor. Do not have anyone else punch you in or out.

USE OF LIBRARY EQUIPMENT AND SUPPLIES

Equipment and supplies are for library business and are not to be used for any personal business without special permission. In general, office equipment is not available for personal use as our space is too congested to accommodate additional work without adversely affecting the daily operations.

COPYING MACHINES AND COPY CARDS

Office copying machines and Departmental copy cards are available for library copying only and are not to be used for any personal copying.

TELEPHONES

Telephones are provided for library business. Except for emergencies, personal calls should be handled using phones outside the office.

WORKSTUDY

Keep your supervisor informed about your workstudy status.

WHERE TO TURN IF YOU HAVE QUESTIONS

If you have questions about pay, benefits, or other matters concerning your employment in the Library check with your immediate supervisor. S/he will be able to get you started in the right direction.

The last page of the brochure is blank, except for the heading "Notes:"; and the outside back cover shows the date the pamphlet was issued: February 1989.

SAMPLE STUDENT EMPLOYEE HANDBOOK FROM A LARGE UNIVERSITY BRANCH LIBRARY

The following text is from the training materials for student employees working in the Engineering Library of the University of California, Berkeley. It was written by Patricia Davitt Maughan, then head of the branch.

GUIDELINES FOR STAFF CONDUCT

RATIONALE

Public Service is our business! Whether you are working in the public service area checking out books or in the workroom updating records, the needs of the patron should be your primary concern. Everything you do in the Engineering Library is related to public service. The attitude you project while on the job and your job performance affect the patrons' confidence in the quality of service to be given.

We expect that everyone is motivated to do a good job. Procedures have been established and are reviewed periodically so that we can all work efficiently as a unit. But no matter how efficient the operation, we will be judged ultimately by the patrons' expectations of the kind of service an academic-oriented library should offer; and expectations are high.

The College of Engineering at Berkeley ranks as one of the most prestigious in the U.S. and attracts students and scholars from around the world. Therefore, each staff member, from the librarian to the student circulation clerk, must exhibit the same high level of professionalism in public service that will project a businesslike atmosphere of efficiency and competence.

The purpose of these guidelines is to remind us that we are not just performing routine tasks, but are working in an environment in which how well we respond to patrons' needs requires the same critical assessment as is given to the performance of routine tasks.

ATTENDANCE AND DEPENDABILITY

One way to demonstrate good relations with your coworkers and the public and a positive attitude toward your job is by being dependable and having a good record of attendance. Scheduling and assignment of duties are based on the needs of the Library and adherence to a prearranged schedule is of the utmost importance. Arriving at work on time, working the total number of hours you are allotted every week, not abusing break privileges, and working efficiently while on the job are all factors used to determine your record of attendance and dependability.

When you fail to work the specific times assigned to you, something or someone suffers: the flow of work is adversely affected, a patron is denied good service because he must wait in a queue, an appointment is not kept, or another staff member's work suffers when others must perform your tasks instead of their own.

Your supervisor will consider your work habits as a statement of your character and willingness to accept responsibility when you are given a performance evaluation. This will become part of your employment record and will be a significant factor to be considered if you seek a recommendation for employment elsewhere.

GENERAL CONDUCT

Please remember that you are working in a setting in which how you conduct yourself often has a direct impact on library patrons and your coworkers. Here are some useful reminders:

1. Keep your voice low. Voices carry far in the Library and loud talking in the workroom can also be heard in the public service areas. Many patrons are in the Library to do research or to study and do not wish to be disturbed—nor do your coworkers who are engaged in work.

2. Your first consideration is always the patron, not the task in hand. Help the patron first; file cards later. Remain aware of patrons seeking your attention. If it appears that a transaction with one patron will take more that a minute or two, acknowledge the waiting patron(s) and offer some reasonable estimate of when assistance will be available. When requests received over the telephone cannot be accommodated because patrons in the library must be served first, it is not unreasonable to explain the situation and ask the patron to call back. In any situation, never leave patrons waiting without an indication that help will be available to them.

3. Personal conversations among staff in the public service areas may convey a number of negative impressions to our users. Please confine socializing and personal telephone calls to your rest or lunch breaks. Visitors or persons calling you at work must be made aware you have work to do. Keep the contact short or make arrangements to meet or phone later. Your best rule is to maintain your workspace as a place where serious business is conducted and take care of personal matters during nonworking hours.

RELATIONS WITH PUBLIC AND CO-WORKERS

We all like to work in a pleasant and congenial atmosphere. Extend to coworkers and patrons the same courtesy and consideration you would expect in return. You will find that a positive attitude has its reward in creating less stressful work relations for everyone, including yourself. We all work under the same conditions and limits on time cause job frustrations, especially when patron demand is high; your supervisor is available to assist you at any time. Be sure to ask for assistance when:

1. additional circulation desk coverage is needed to handle peak workload periods
2. relief is needed for rest or lunch breaks
3. patron demands exceed your job responsibility
4. or any time you feel it is necessary or advisable.

If an incident occurs in which you feel you have been wrongly treated by a patron or a coworker, refer the matter to your supervisor, who can usually take corrective action. Every attempt will be made to remedy the situation as soon as possible.

DRESS AND PERSONAL MANNER

Patrons are sensitive to both dress and manners. While there is no dress code for the Engineering Library, you are expected to use some discretion and wear clothes to work that are both comfortable and appropriate to the kind of activity that occurs in an academic library. What is suitable attire for your auto repair or physical education class is not considered suitable for the Library. For safety reasons, shoes are required.

Your pleasant and efficient manner when dealing with patrons will project a positive attitude toward the Library and the services offered here. An impatient tone of voice, a distracted facial expression, or kicking back in a chair with your feet up do not offer the patron much confidence in the quality of service to be given.

As a library employee, your actions are often visible while working in public areas; your dress and personal manner should be in keeping with the friendly, cooperative, and businesslike image we wish to project.

STAFF WORKROOM

Public awareness should extend to the staff workroom; the kind of attitude and work habits you cultivate in the office can easily be transmitted into the public service areas of the library.

Talking or visiting while in the workroom is likely to disturb those who must give their full attention to completing tasks or assignments. Remember that workspace is limited and is shared; please be sensitive to the effects that office conversation have on your own productivity, patron response, and the work of others.

Kitchen privileges are extended to all staff on the condition that each staff member take responsibility for cleaning up. All dishes should be washed and put away after use so that the countertop will be clean and clear for the next person's use.

COMMUNICATION

A large part of your job is to impart information to the library users. Whether it is to report on the status of a book not on the shelf, to assist in the interpretation of a holding record, or to point to where the restrooms are, you are often the only contact the patron has with the Library. The goal is to give each patron the best possible service. The following suggestions should help you to communicate effectively:

1. Remember you are serving a diverse clientele with different informational needs. Rephrase questions if necessary to help you determine what it is the patron really wants to know. For example, if the patron asks whether the Library is open in the evenings, a simple affirmative answer is insufficient; what the patron may want to know is the schedule of closing times, which vary from day to day.

2. A simple question may require more than a simple answer if there is an indica-

tion that the patron is unfamiliar with the Library and how it operates. To answer "The TK's are on the upper level" is not helpful since it does not really tell the patron how to find call numbers on the shelves. It would be more informative to add "All of the call numbers are in alphanumeric order on the shelves" so the patron will know how to proceed in finding the material needed.

3. Allow time to complete information transactions. It may be necessary to repeat information or instructions, especially if the patron does not understand English well. Be patient and courteous at all times; if you feel pressured and cannot adequately handle the level of patron demand, don't take it out on the patron. Call upon your supervisor for assistance.

4. Refer patrons to the Information Desk or to other appropriate sources when lengthy instruction is required, for example: how to use Catalogs 1 & 2, how to look up technical reports, or how to search in abstracts and indexes. The time you take in these activities takes time away from the duties to which you are assigned; it is important that you put your own duties first.

5. Use library terminology sparingly. Be descriptive of any jargon you do use—a patron will only understand what a "shelflist" is if you explain its purpose.

6. Avoid extending your answer beyond your specific knowledge or expertise. Misinformation is wasteful of a patron's time (and yours!) and may cut the user off from other important resources that may be available. When you don't know or are not sure of an answer, or when you are not expected to know the answer, refer the question to your supervisor or the staff member who has the special skills to answer the question.

CONCLUSION

The work of each member of the Library staff is of vital importance to the consistent provision of quality service to library users. Following the guidelines above will ensure that the Engineering Library will continue to provide the friendly, efficient, and professional service that is expected by our patrons.

INDEX